PUTTING MY ASH ON THE LINE

poems by

Kathleen Holliday

Finishing Line Press
Georgetown, Kentucky

PUTTING MY ASH ON THE LINE

Dedicated to
my family
&
in memoriam:
Richard (Rick) C. Nelson
John R. Mitchell
Faculty of Augsburg University
&
Diego and Zandor
who would have loved these poems
if each one had been crumpled into a ball
for them to play with
&
to the one who asked,
"So, do you send these out?"

These poems are composed of material sustainably harvested
from certified old growth.

Copyright © 2020 by Kathleen Holliday
ISBN 978-1-64662-373-0 First Edition
All rights reserved under International and Pan-American Copyright Conventions. No part of this book may be reproduced in any manner whatsoever without written permission from the publisher, except in the case of brief quotations embodied in critical articles and reviews.

ACKNOWLEDGMENTS

Grateful acknowledgment to the editors of the following publications in which these poems, some in slightly different versions, first appeared:

The Bellingham Review: "The Spawning Imperative"
The Blue Nib Literary Magazine: "Putting My Ash on the Line," "Hurly-burly"
Cathexis Northwest Press: "A Great White," "A Long-Standing Engagement," "The Boys of Summer"
Cathexis Northwest Press Our Poetica, an anthology: "Caterfamilias"
Common Ground Review, "Post-Impressionism" (Honorable Mention, CGR Poetry Contest 2019)
Poetry Super Highway, "For One Night Only," "Indoor Life"
SHARK REEF, A Literary Magazine: "A Little Green," "Memento Mori," "Ms. Havisham," "Subsidence," "To the Light" (forthcoming)
The Write Launch, "The Weighing of the Heart," "The Wine-Dark Sea"

My heartfelt thanks to the Women Writers of the Salish Sea: Suzanne Berry, Brooks, Marty Clark, Iris Graville, Rita Larom, Ann Norman, Lorna Reese and Gretchen Wing for their guidance, insights, and generosity. I am honored to be in the company of such literary citizens.

Publisher: Leah Maines
Editor: Christen Kincaid
Cover Art: Karlena Pickering, KP5 Photography,
        https://www.facebook.com/kp5photography/
Author Photo: Robert S. Harrison, www.rsharrison.com
Cover Design: Elizabeth Maines McCleavy

Order online: www.finishinglinepress.com
      also available on amazon.com

Author inquiries and mail orders:
Finishing Line Press
P. O. Box 1626
Georgetown, Kentucky 40324
U. S. A.

Table of Contents

- Putting My Ash on the Line 1
- Caterfamilias 3
- Fleuron 4
- The Joy of Text 5
- A Long-Standing Engagement 7
- Thanksgiving 8
- The Bounty 9
- Post-Impressionism 10
- Indoor Life 12
- The Wine-Dark Sea 13
- Hurly-burly 14
- Love in a Hot Climate 15
- For One Night Only 16
- A Little Green 17
- A Great White 18
- Memento Mori 20
- Bag Lady 21
- The Boys of Summer 22
- A Closer Reading of the Text 23
- Ms. Havisham 24
- Closing Time 26
- The Spawning Imperative 27
- A Day like That 28
- Going for the Jocular 29
- The Deer at the Door 31
- Lascaux 32
- To the Light 33
- Subsidence 34
- The Weighing of the Heart 35

Putting My Ash on the Line
Poetry is just the evidence of your life.
If your life is burning well, poetry is just the ash. Leonard Cohen

Sometimes, I find piles
from little volcanoes
like the remains of cone incense,
a wisp of smoke in the air:
reductio ad absurdum, or,

an aromatic lump of ambergris,
a flake of alchemist's gold,

the ends of papers curling up,

the pugilist pose of a body
seized by extreme heat.

Set afire by others too:
turning round and round,
a firework sputtering, then
blurring into a single flame.

from the radiance of other conflagrations,
a sustaining heat to warm my hands;

my mother's ashes in my cupboard
still glowing.

And even in last night's dream,
I poled among the delta reeds
as flaming scraps—papyri,
rained down into the water
hissing;

I trimmed my oars
and stood, reaching up
to smear my face and hands
with the falling ash
of an ancient library
burning.

On waking, I pray:
let me be fire,
let me be wood.

Caterfamilias

A poem paws me awake.
Softly insistent, it takes me
by the scruff of my neck
lifts me out of bed

drops me gently
onto the chair at the table,
in front of the pen and the page
beneath the golden glow
of the lamp.

There it curls up on my lap.
yawns,
leaving me
to do all the work
translating
its resonant purr.

Fleuron

In that pre-digital life
in the art library,
I felt like an obituarian,
tending to those painters,
sculptors, photographers,
typographers and others,
from whom no more works of art
would appear except
posthumously.

They lay with the still living,
interred in blond oak drawers
like miniature coroner trays.

I crooked an index finger
under the brass hook,
pulled out the wooden drawer,
unscrewed the brass rod
that held the cards in place;
discarded the old, inserted the update,
and as the drawer fit neatly home,

imagined a fleuron blooming
like a tiny black wreath,
on every card, where the brackets
of birth and death had closed.

The Joy of Text
(or, Librarians Only Make Reference to it)

A back-lit screen is not the same
as lit from within.

I'd rather read a thick book
hold its tome-escent weight
turn pages splotched with
another reader's dried pizza sauce
feel the scales of my hands
tip left as the hours pass.

There's no scrolling down
no swiping, no pinching a screen.
The only zooming in
zooming out
is when I remove
then put my glasses
back on.

Oh, Simon & Schuster (& all those others)
you had me at colophon!
So many bodies of work
leave me breathless.
As a writer, I confess
to longing for my very own
ISBN number.

I never tire of reading a
Dedication (to this book, I commit myself)
Call number (so I'll know where to find you
and others like you again)

Preface (that literary trailer)

In Gratitude (I'm glad all those folks
helped you write this book, too)

Footnote (those divinely distracting
rabbit holes where de facto,
I learn a little Latin),

and, for more,
be still my beating heart,
there's a Bibliography!

How I savor a serifed font
delight in a deckle-edged page
luxuriate in the joy of text,
imprinted for life

and at THE END
bask in the afterglow
of Afterword:

kindled.

Perfectly bound to every
book I've ever read.

A Long-Standing Engagement

Of the three of us sisters,
I'm the only one
unmarried, undivorced.
"You dodged that bullet,"
my older sister says,
though I count it as two.
Still, I don't think of myself
as target practice.

Why is it, when I think of married life,
it's William Burroughs and his wife:
"Stand still, my dear.
 Trust me?"

Much safer, perhaps, to live in sin
(venial, menial or mortal),
shack up,
without benefit of clergy.
I wouldn't need a diamond as big as the Ritz.
I could live with you and be your love,
and we could all the bookish pleasures prove.

As time goes by—
less Cirque du Soleil,
more sea lions basking on a beach;
I could bring two books to bed
one for us each.

But I have to say
I plighted my troth early
like that teenage Capulet,
though my engagement's lasted
much longer than hers;
spoken for a long time ago
by that murmur in my ears,
the sweet somethings
I keep writing down:
Forever Yours,
in all these words.

Thanksgiving

This holiday I'm thankful for
a family member's methadone
instead of heroin,

another's cold turkey
sobriety and new-found
partnerhood,

another's I.D. in time to vote
despite no permanent home,

for missing that deer
while I drove to another funeral,

and every Thanksgiving
since her death
my mother's recipe
for pumpkin pie.

The Bounty
To My Father

You so admired Captain Bligh,
a sailor like you.
"3600 miles in an open boat—
what seamanship!"
you declared at dinner.

And the crew that set him adrift?

"Well, those bastards got what they deserved,"
spoken from the captain's chair,
head of the family.

Around the table
your wife and children sat,
eyes averted,
cutlery at the ready,
mutinous.

Had we known what lay ahead,
our voyage might have ended
with your burial at sea.

Post-Impressionism

There has always been
so much to read—
by the age of nine,
my eyes were overwhelmed.

Though I swept and swept
the floor, my father wrested
the broom from my hands,
beat me with it, swept me
out of the kitchen:
"Don't tell me you
can't see that dirt!"

Not long after, I came home
clutching a note from my
teacher that read:
"Kathy can't see the blackboard."

At the optometrist's office
I sat multi-lensed like a fly:
click, click, click, click
click, click, click, click
click,
until I could see not just the big E
but the grain of wood paneling,
the mosaic of asphalt on the freeway home,
my own eyes reflected
back at me in thick lenses;
lashes batting,
startled by clarity.

Above the walnut-veneered buffet,
what I'd taken as a portrait
of my mother and older sister
in rain-fresh blues and greens,
a title at the bottom of the frame,
revealed to be, *On The Terrace*;
from a smear of yellow,
a name: Renoir.

My mother's face came into focus:
so worn, so drawn,
so much older;

the thousand-yard stare
of her aquamarine eyes.

That first moment
I saw her world,
I had to look away.

Indoor Life

Among those things my father
kept within easy reach, I remember:

a round glass ashtray, walnut pipe rack,
foam-edged beer glass on the lamp table,

boxes of red shotgun shells
under the full gun rack,

a black leather belt on a hook
near the back door,

back issues of Guns & Ammo,
American Rifleman and Outdoor Life.

I flipped through to a feature story.
The hairs on the back of my neck rose

as I read of a grizzly
that tore off a hunter's scalp
and most of his face,

clawed his torso,
ripped his shoulder open.

The hunter lay still, played dead.
The bear buried him

under dirt and leaves,
left him alive,
to tell the story.

I slipped the magazine back
where I'd found it

and considered how I might
survive this indoor life.

The Wine-Dark Sea

A sea wife,
my mother didn't have time
to pace a widow's walk,
searching for a sail on the horizon.

She was too busy
pinning up sheets to dry,
weeding the garden,
kneading floury bread dough,
wrangling four children.

No suitors to fend off.
No weaving to unpick.
She knitted argyle socks
for her Odysseus.

After a shift at the cannery
she sat up late tapping
on the old Remington
the songs she'd written
in her head while sorting
green beans for Del Monte.

Did she ever wonder
if a Circe waited
at some exotic port,
if he ever answered a siren's call?

For nearly twenty years,
she heard the Trojan stories,
every pub crawl and brawl
from Ithaca to Yokohama retold.

When he retired from a life at sea,
to his pipe, his dog, his guns,
his wife and children,
to reclaim his throne-like chair,

her once-familiar stranger
brought home the war.

Hurly-burly

Oh, I wish we were three again:
Phyllis and her daughters,
sitting around that kitchen table,
steam from our coffee cups
braiding up with our cigarette smoke
to the ceiling,

Oh, I wish we were there again
in that little blue and white house
with the lace curtain over the window
cut from my sister's wedding dress,
after the divorce,

for her to scratch off a lotto ticket—
winning just enough for a new muffler
for the undead Dodge parked outside.

For her to lean in, over the
salt and pepper shakers,
a conspirator once more, to say,
 "When shall we three meet again?"

For her daughters to catch her eye,
for us to cackle like hell.

Of this I'm sure: we'll meet again,
when this hurly-burly's done.

Love in a Hot Climate

We were living together
when he so casually described
his ideal woman—
petite and dark
Jewish, he said, or perhaps Puerto Rican
whose stiletto heels might click across
the floor like castanets.

Later, after we'd parted
he showed a photo
of his new love
saying how much, to his surprise
she looked like me.

He never even closed his book
when two women left the room
on silent, sandaled feet.

For One Night Only

There was a poet
now dead
who once danced me backwards
into his bedroom.

We leaned as one,
in a too-many-beers tango—
my Ginger to his Fred
without the heels
and filmy gown—

just three steps forward:
approach
affinity
wild abandon

not thinking of tomorrow's
two steps back:
avoidance
then abandonment.

I thought our cues were taken
from the same film—
perhaps, *An Affair to Remember,*
or was it, *A Night to Remember?*

Sure enough, the morning after
my ticket stub was stamped the latter.
Not just Titanic
steerage.

If we'd agreed on another film
something a bit less tragic
no Oscar Werner, no Simone Signoret
it still would play for one night only
Ship of Fools.

A Little Green
    (for Daphne)

I hoped to burst into leaf
(having read it worked for her),
my toes sunk deep into brown carpet,
arms branching toward the ceiling—
a little green,
a thicker skin.

Did she turn in time
to feel his arms surround a slender bole
embracing her still-racing heart?

I believe she was the only one
who got away.

A Great White

Heaving up out of the sea
your body breached,
a white flash of underbelly,
a gleaming row of hooks embedded in your lips:
all those bonds you'd managed to break free of
or took with you
sounding,
drowning them.

My line, dangling down into the deep,
you once swallowed whole
in a fine display of teeth.
In your wake
my little coracle flooded,
sank, tipping me into the drink
with you.

In those sightings that followed,
I could never tell if what I saw was
a cetacean, its heart well-insulated,
its song an echo in my blood,
not fully understood,

or a cold-blooded shadow
flicking a tail, gliding over
rippled sand in the ocean floor,
appetite indiscriminate,
driven only to keep moving.

There, below the surface,
I suffered a sea change.
Washed ashore,
I learned to walk
with the ghost of a limb.

Here, on this island of memory,
what I recall of that time at sea:
I was never close enough,

my arm never strong enough
to sink a lance;

My hands could never hold
the salt water that fell
from my eyes,

My story, no simple tale
of a fish, or the need
for a bigger boat.

Memento Mori

> *After great pain, a formal feeling comes.*
> *—Emily Dickinson*

It is time for putting away—and yet,
an aura lingers over a photograph,
a card or two.

Of himself, there is hardly a sign;
red roses in the vase blacken
and drop to the floor as if to say:
Don't expect a miracle.

Were I able to address him
only Latin words would fall
unfurling from my mouth
like the penitent in a medieval frieze
for whom a saint is forever interceding.

Bag Lady

A homeless man pushing a cart
stops to watch our chance meeting—
I rest my grocery bags on the snow,
your arms circle me,
my arms stretch up, around you,
a bear in winter
wearing a wool watch-cap;
your coat like a pelt, belted,
your scarf I knitted that by now
could really use a wash.

We hold the moment so long
the bystander exclaims,
"That's a helluva hug!"

He couldn't know
we were by then,
living apart.

After they left,
no one saw me
gather up my bags,
hugging to myself
the memory of home.

The Boys of Summer

> *"They are leaning out for love,*
> *and they will lean that way forever."*   Leonard Cohen

My feet push off the ground
tipping,
way, way back.
I wonder just how far
I can lean in my new
lounge chair.

I could lean this way
forever,
falling back into other summers,
weightless,

until I'm brought up short by my age.
Gravity socks me firmly
in its palm like a ball
in a catcher's mitt,

but not before I remember
all the leaning out for love,
longing for someone
to catch me.

A Closer Reading of the Text

To me
he will always be
a slim volume
of poetry
in a fine Italian hand

which eludes
a closer reading
of the text.

And I to him?
A work of fiction
a mystery enthralling
unforgettable
well-written

a library edition
returned to circulation
unread.

Ms. Havisham

I, too, had great expectations.
To be or not to be a wife
defined my life.

My dowry guaranteed
 a husband, and I would be
a mother, helpmeet, nurse.
Nothing could be worse than
that damning epithet:
old maid.

Left at the altar—jilted.
My bouquet wilting,
I drew my veil down over my face
and let the yards of lace fall
dragging through the dust.

Years later, I still hold the knife:
May I cut you a slice—
a corner piece perhaps, with extra icing?
Don't mind the spiders
and the mice racing in and out,
tunnels crumbling behind them.

Mr. Dickens, I implore you—
change mine to a happy ending.
No funeral pyre,
no more desires gone up in smoke.
Set me in some future time
when I could say:
never married,
never needed to;
earned a degree, had a job, a car,
a condo in the city,
a lover who never strayed.

I'd celebrate my singular good fortune
with a cake—
not Mrs. Beeton's recipe—
no butter, no gluten, no nuts.
I'd clear up after with a cordless vac.

I'd sweep the ceiling free of spider webs.
I'd read a novel in one sitting
then I'd take a nap.

Closing Time

Now that I live in the country
there's no doorbell to ring.
The motion sensor spotlights
a raccoon, unsteadily upright,
sidling like a drunk after closing time.

Hanging on the door handle, swaying,
he squints into my living room,
Not my house,
and staggers away.

There are nights I wonder
what other shapes could emerge
out of the dark, suddenly revealed.

There are nights I wonder
how different my life might have been
had I always kept the animal out;

how much less trouble
in the morning light
to wipe paw prints
off the door.

The Spawning Imperative

A long time ago
we stood belly-up to the bar
jostling for elbow room
calling out drinks to the barman.
Above, in the convex mirror
our reflection:
a waterfall cascading
salmon
arched and twisting,
leaping higher and higher
for the spawning ground.

What now, I wonder.

I could set the oven on broil
garnish with parsley
place a lemon slice like a coin
over the staring eye
but then it winks at me
and the tail slaps down
on the bamboo cutting board
inviting me to remember
the open sea.

A Day like That

A French tower guard
stood stupefied by the vision
of dragon-headed prows
cleaving the river mist—
a Viking fleet, 100 strong,
churning closer, up the Seine.

In the scriptorium,
clerestory windows to the sky,
I breathed life into a tissue
a fluttering of gold leaf
and with a bone stylus,
carefully, tenderly,
about to affix it to the page
when all the church bells of Paris
rang out the alarum:
"Lord, save us from these pagan devils!"

My hand slipped,
the gold leaf crumpled
to a yellow spitball. *Merde.*

It was a day like that.

Going for the Jocular

A DNA test confirms
my ethnic ancestry.
Small wonder I feel the cold
and damp from generations spent
in rainy climes
icy fjords
an emerald isle.

Even at several removes
some traits still manifest:

all that Englishness
phlegmatic, apologetic
Sorry! Sorry!

a Scandinavian dourness
that would leave Ibsen envious
a once-beserker mode tamed
to manic attacks of cleaning
Uff da!

and enough Irishness to instill
a certain going for the jocular
despite all indications to the contrary.
Jayzus!

Take this story for example:
A woman walks into a bar...
Ok, not that one, how about this?
When you left
it was *all* my fault,
that glass not merely empty
but hammered into dust, my sight
eclipsed to black.
I consoled myself:
someday this will all be
feckin' hilarious
or I'll be dead

and it won't matter.

I'm still waiting
for the laugh on that one.

Perhaps we'll meet again
in hell.

Oh, pardon me, after you.
And save me a seat, will ya?

Ah. Finally,
warm enough.

The Deer at the Door

The doe is back after the long winter
nosing the window-paneled door
leaving a smudge like a kiss
seeking out the cats who
jumped down from the loveseat
to chatter at her,
their conversation
a communion of creatures.

She strides to another windowpane,
then another,
peering in for signs of life;
there's only the halting motion of my hand
guiding the pen across the page.

She wasn't here when the vet came,
when the wind off the water cut like a knife,
when I laid their bodies gently in the earth
under the pine tree I can see from where I sit.

I wish I had some way to tell her,
they won't be back.

Lascaux

Hunkered down in my cave
this winter morning
I wait for sunrise.

At the flip of a switch
fire erupts in the gas fireplace.
I stare into the living flames,
pictures flung around
in shadowy relief:

Hatch marks painted in ash—
every year not smoking,
my own years tallied,
each new one
an exclamation.

Images of my clan—
the dancing spears
over the body of the mastodon—
how we feasted that Thanksgiving!

Totems of my hunting companions,
the sabre-toothed ones,
gone now—where?

One hand raised against the dark,
fingers spread wide.
An outline traced—

these daubs in ochre,
blood,
charcoal,
ink,

something of me
to remain behind.

To the Light

Because of,
or perhaps despite
my whisperings,
the African violet thrives.

When I woke this morning,
my heart daunted by what
we humans keep doing
to other humans,

there it was:
a bud that wasn't there yesterday,
topping a pale stem in a whorl of green,

a tiny fist raised
to the light.

Subsidence

Like a thatched cottage
on a windswept isle
abandoned,
this edifice too, will settle,
sink slowly, thistle-deep
into loam.

Someday an archaeological intern
may smooth away the moss
with soft brushes,
unearth the artifacts of this life:
empty pen barrels,
a shard of Blue Willow bowl,
spines of books articulating what was read,
soles of shoes stopped in their striding.

All of which may sprout academic theories
as to the manner of this emigrant's
last look of home—

turfed out by that implacable landlord?

a sudden withering blight?

or after a long, tumultuous voyage,
with sails luffing, going hull down
over the horizon to that
undiscovered country
from which no traveler returns?

If left alone long enough, the strata
might be harvested in oblongs,
rolled and stacked
ready for laying down in a grate
in a room where voices sing,
fiddles and drums play,

to warm a cold night.

The Weighing of the Heart

When my heart is placed
on the scales
against Ma'at's feather—
or perhaps a quill,

when I no longer have eyes to see,
no breath to hold
waiting for the judgment,

will Anubis standing by,
press his thumb on the tray
where my heart lies,
lift it out and toss it

to the crocodile-headed goddess
who will snap up the tender morsel
in her jaws?

Or will I be handed back
the boarding pass of my heart
along with all I'll ever need
pulled behind me
like wheeled luggage,

every canopic jar ringing
a harmonic at the gateway
to the After Life?

Born in the Pacific Northwest, Kathleen once lived on a farm near Mount St. Helens. She spent over twenty years in Minnesota before returning home to Washington State. She was attending a sister's wedding about 30 miles from the volcano when it erupted. But that's a story all its own.

After graduating from Augsburg University in Minneapolis, Kathleen worked variously as executive secretary to an occult publisher, a tarot reader, a typesetter, and a proofreader before finding a niche in academic libraries, and, later, as an academic counselor at the University of Washington. Most recently she served as a library assistant at a small, rural, public library. While stereotypes of library staffers abound, it's safe to say Kathleen reads a lot.

She lives and writes on an island in the Salish Sea in Washington State accessible only by ferry. It's a landscape of stunning natural beauty like that found only in fantasy tales: the Shire perhaps, or Lothlorien. Once again, she finds herself living where another dormant volcano, Mt. Baker, looms on the horizon.